Published by Grolier Books, a division of Grolier Enterprises Inc.

Disney Presents The Wonderful World of Knowledge
ISBN 0-7172-8929-X
Painting and Sculpture ISBN 0-7172-8948-6

First published in 1999

Printed and bound in China by
Toppan Printing Company

Originated in Italy by Articolor

Designed and compiled by
Marshall Editions Developments Limited

GROLIER
BOOKS

The Wonderful World of Knowledge

Painting and Sculpture

Using The Wonderful World of Knowledge

Mickey, Minnie, Donald, Daisy, Goofy, and Pluto are ready to take you on an adventure ride through the world of learning. Discover the secrets of science, nature, our world, the past, and much more. Climb aboard and enjoy the ride.

Look here for a general summary of the theme

Labels tell *you what's happening in the pictures*

The pictures by *themselves can tell you a lot, even before you read a word*

Mickey's ears *lead you to one of the main topics*

Watch out for special pages where Mickey takes a close look at some key ideas

The Solar Sys

The Solar System is th
given to our Sun and its fa
planets. It also includes th
moons, millions of pieces c
called asteroids and meteo
and frozen lumps of dust a
called comets. Everything c
can see in the sky is outsid
Solar System and is far, far
away. Every single star is
itself a sun, and each may
have its own family of
planets and moons.

Saturn is surrounded by beautiful rings

REPTILES AND AMPHIBIANS

Color and Camouflage

Frogs and toads come in nearly every imaginable color, even gold or black. They have a wide range of patterns, from spots and stripes to zigzags.

Color and pattern help frogs and toads survive. Bright colors warn that they may be poisonous. Drab colors camouflage them, or hide them against their background. Many tree frogs are exactly the same green as leaves, while others look like bark. The Asian horned toad has the best camouflage of all. Folds of patchy, brown skin and a flat body make it look like a dead leaf when it lies still on the forest floor.

Folds of brown skin *give perfect camouflage*

Flat body is hard *to see among dead leaves*

Asian horned toad

False-eyed frog

Markings *look like eyes*

For extra *protection, bad-smelling liquid oozes out around false eyes*

FALSE-EYED FROG
The South American false-eyed frog has large markings on its flanks that look like eyes. These fool some predators into thinking that they are looking at a much larger animal, such as a cat or bird.

COLOR AND CAMOUFLAGE

Dog sniffing *curiously at the toad*

Oriental fire-bellied toad defending itself against a dog

Skin oozes *a stinging fluid*

Bright *colored belly*

Green and *black back*

Toad rears up *on its back legs*

FIRE-BELLIED TOAD
When cornered by a predator, the Oriental fire-bellied toad of eastern Asia arches its back and rears up on its legs to show its fiery underside. Wise attackers back off, because the toad's skin oozes a stinging, bad-tasting fluid.

Strawberry arrow frog

POISON-DART FROGS
Deadly poison oozes from the skin of Central and South American poison-dart frogs. People in the rain forest rub the tips of their arrows and blowpipe darts on the skin of these frogs to collect the poison to use for hunting.

Blue poison-dart frog

FIND OUT MORE
MAMMALS: Camouflage
PLANET EARTH: Forests

16

17

Mickey's page *numbers help you look things up. Don't forget there's a glossary and index at the back of each book*

Goofy and his *friends know how to give you a chuckle on every topic*

Mickey points you to more information in other books in your *The Wonderful World of Knowledge*

FIND OUT MORE
MAMMALS: Camouflage
PLANET EARTH: Forests

AMAZING FACTS
★ The Sun is enormous compared to the planets. It is nearly 1,000 times more massive than the giant planet Jupiter.
Your favorite characters present some facts to astound you and your friends
THE SOLAR SYSTEM
HOW OUR SOLAR SYSTEM WAS FORMED
1 The Solar System formed 4.6 billion years ago. It started at the center of an enormous swirling cloud of gas and dust
2 The Sun burst into flames and became a star. Its light and warmth spread throughout the new Solar System
3 Gas and dust left over from making the Sun clumped together in places. These clumps grew bigger and formed the planets
4 The planets closest to the Sun are small and made from rock and metal. The larger outer planets are made from gas and liquid
Numbers lead you step-by-step through how things happen
Pluto is the farthest planet from the Sun
Each planet has its own path, or orbit
Planet orbits
ORBITING THE SUN
No matter how still you try to be, you are always moving. This is because the Earth – and all the other planets – are moving. They are flying through Space around the Sun in looping paths called orbits
Colorful boxes zoom in on information
Neptune is a cold, blue planet
Uranus is tipped over on its side
THE "PULL" OF GRAVITY
If you throw a ball into the air, it comes down again. The invisible force that pulls it down to Earth is called gravity. The Earth's gravity holds us down on the ground. The Sun's gravity is strong enough to hold all its planets in their orbits
Gravity pulls a ball to Earth
FIND OUT MORE
PLANET EARTH: Night and day
SCIENCE ALL AROUND US: Gravity
The Solar System
Mickey's helpers test some ideas themselves

Contents

INTRODUCING

Painting and Sculpture

The first artists drew pictures on the walls of their caves. Later artists looked around them for materials. They sculpted with stone and wood, decorated with feathers and seashells, and molded metals and clay.

Many painters and sculptors of the past honored gods and rulers and celebrated great events. Today's artists create works for our pleasure, often using the exciting ideas and products of modern times – videos and lasers, concrete, and plastics.

Stone Age Art

The first paintings and sculptures were made around 30,000 years ago, long before paper or metal carving tools had been invented. Stone Age paintings have been found on rocks and on cave walls in Europe, Africa, and Australia. Many of them show the wild animals early people hunted for food. These pictures may have been made in the hope that they would work as magic and make the animals easier to catch.

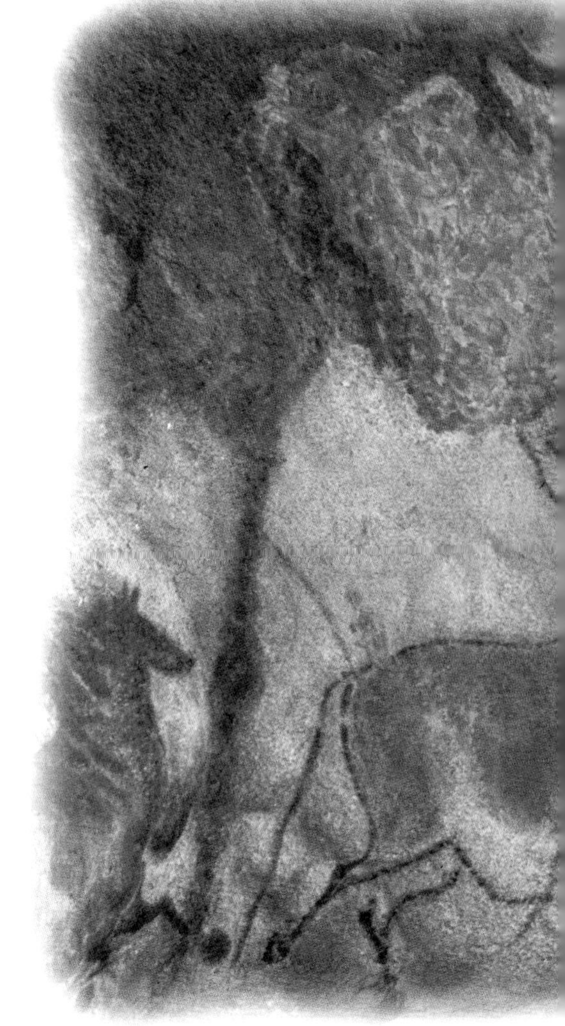

STONE AGE SCULPTURES

Some of the earliest sculptures are small figures of people. They are made from stone, bone, ivory, and clay and may have been carried around as magic charms. These figures are often of women and use simple shapes and lines.

Sculpture of woman's head in ivory, c. 22,000 B.C.

LASCAUX CAVES

Horses, bulls, and other animals were painted in caves at Lascaux in France. Paint was made by crushing colored rocks into a powder and mixing the powder with water. Sticks or soft pads of moss were used as brushes.

AMAZING FACTS

★ The 17,000-year-old cave paintings at Lascaux were discovered by accident in 1940 by four French boys looking for their lost dog.

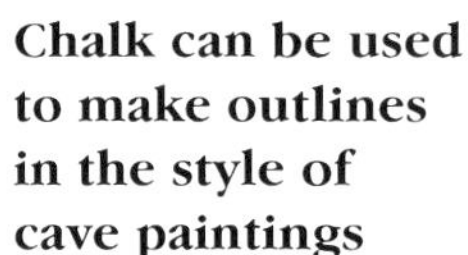

Chalk can be used to make outlines in the style of cave paintings

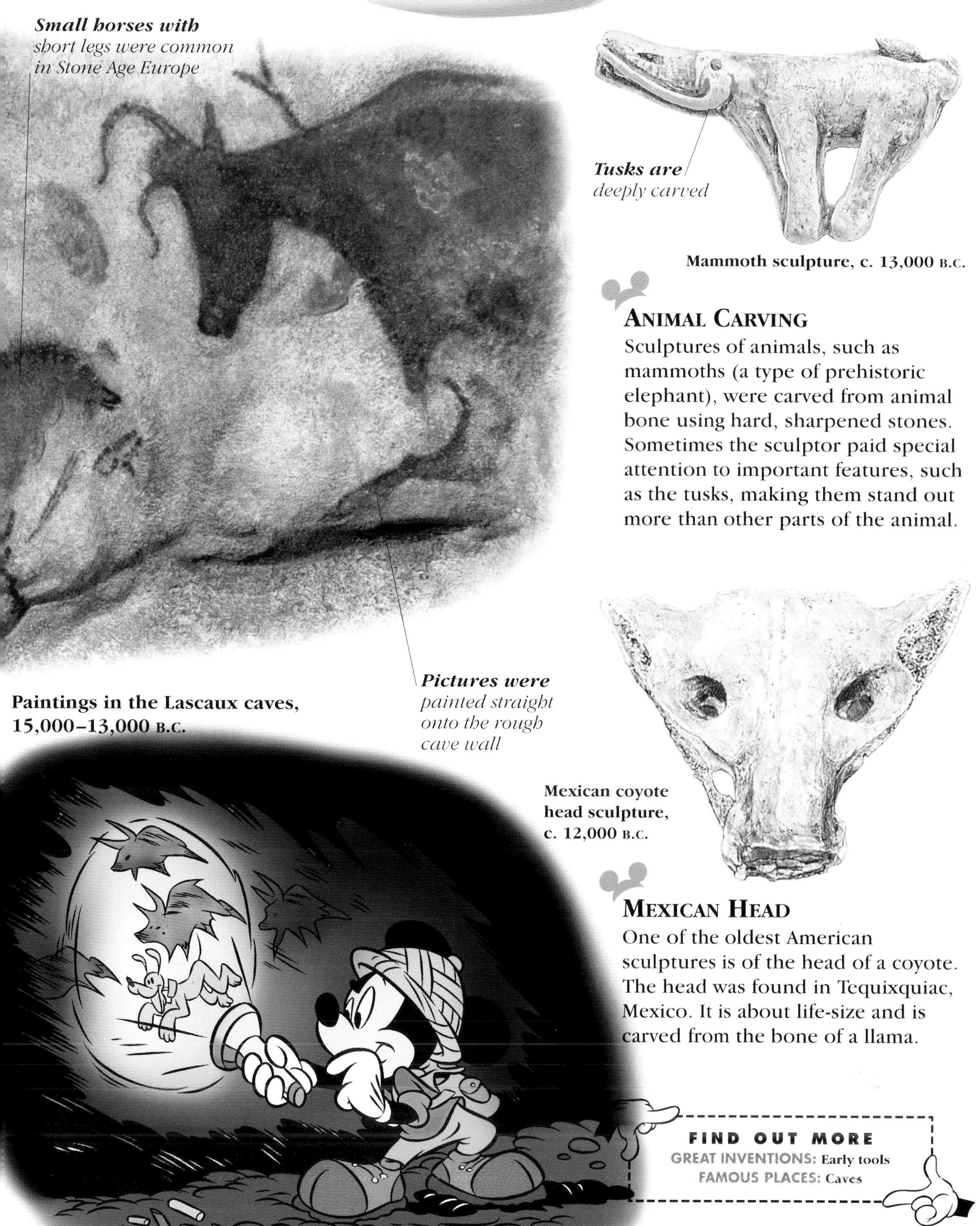
Small horses with short legs were common in Stone Age Europe
Tusks are deeply carved
Pictures were painted straight onto the rough cave wall

Mammoth sculpture, c. 13,000 B.C.

Paintings in the Lascaux caves, 15,000–13,000 B.C.

Mexican coyote head sculpture, c. 12,000 B.C.

ANIMAL CARVING

Sculptures of animals, such as mammoths (a type of prehistoric elephant), were carved from animal bone using hard, sharpened stones. Sometimes the sculptor paid special attention to important features, such as the tusks, making them stand out more than other parts of the animal.

MEXICAN HEAD

One of the oldest American sculptures is of the head of a coyote. The head was found in Tequixquiac, Mexico. It is about life-size and is carved from the bone of a llama.

FIND OUT MORE
GREAT INVENTIONS: Early tools
FAMOUS PLACES: Caves

Traditional Aboriginal and Oceanic Art

The early peoples of Australia and the Pacific Islands used all kinds of natural materials for their art, such as shells, feathers, wood, stone, bark, and seeds. The first Australians, called Aborigines, made pictures on rocks, on the ground, and on flattened sheets of tree bark. The Hawaiian islanders made religious images from feathers, shells, and dog teeth. Often, this early art was made to honor gods or the spirits of ancestors.

Male and female *figures look like dancing skeletons*

Aboriginal "X-ray" rock art at Nourlangie Rock, Australia, c. 14,000 B.C.

Maori house-post carving

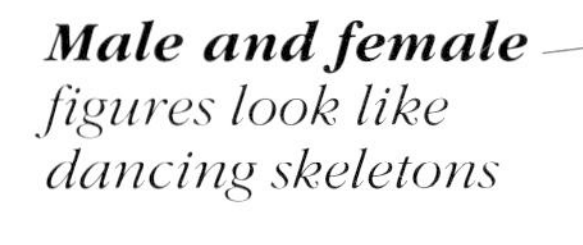

MAORI CARVING

The Maori people of New Zealand decorated their wooden houses and everyday objects with patterns of curving lines and spirals. They also carved images of figures that represented, or stood for, their ancestors.

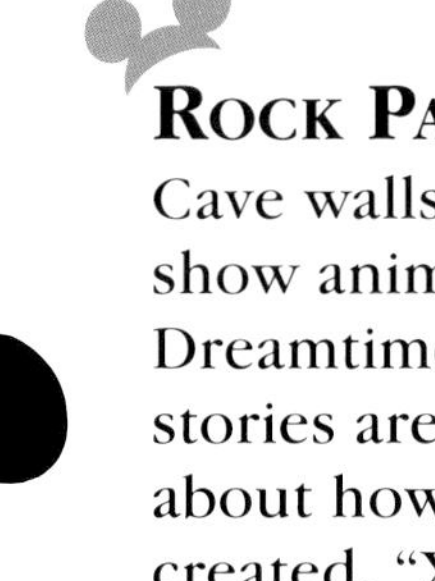

ROCK PAINTING

Cave walls of Aboriginal art show animals and people from Dreamtime stories. These stories are based on beliefs about how the world was created. "X-ray paintings" show an outline of Dreamtime figures as well as the skeleton and parts inside. They look a little like hospital X-ray images.

AMAZING FACTS

★ **Many Pacific islanders decorated their bodies with permanent patterns called tattoos. The skin was pricked in patterns then dyed. Sometimes their whole bodies were covered in designs.**

Row of uneven *square shapes make the fish's backbone*

EASTER ISLAND STATUES

Long ago, the people of Easter Island in the South Pacific put up hundreds of massive, stone figures near the coast. The figures may have been made to remember and respect dead chiefs. The statues' huge bodies and staring eyes make them look like noble creatures from another world.

Huge red stone *cylinders balance on the statue's head, like a hat*

Engraved lines *on long earlobes may represent the chief's ear decorations*

Easter Island statues date from A.D. 1000–1500, and reach heights of 12 m (40 ft)

BARK CLOTH

The Pacific islanders made cloth from tree bark. They colored the cloth with dyes or mud and decorated it with paintings, stencils, or repeated patterns made with small bamboo stamps. Sometimes they even hung the cloth in a smoky place to color it.

Different designs on bark cloth, A.D. 1856

FEATHERED GOD

Featherwork was highly prized by Hawaiian islanders. In battles, warriors carried feathered images of their gods, and chiefs wore feather cloaks. Images of gods were made from feathers fixed to light, basketlike frames. Pearly shells were often used for eyes.

Red was the *color of the gods*

Hawaiian war god, made before A.D. 1779

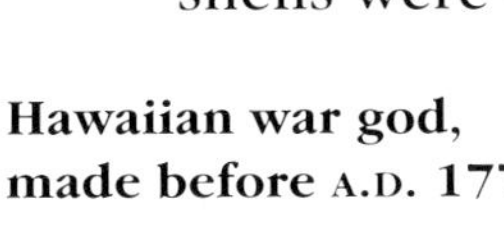

FIND OUT MORE
CHILDREN OF THE WORLD: Australia
FAMOUS PLACES: Uluru

Ancient Art of Central America

The civilizations that once ruled Mexico and Central America produced many kinds of art. The first peoples to rule Mexico were the Olmecs, from about 1200 B.C. to 400 B.C., who made sculptures with rounded shapes. The Maya, who ruled central Mexico from A.D. 250 to 900, left many examples of their art. In the Mexican city-state of Teotihuacán, flatter sculptures with regular patterns of squares and circles were made. Each civilization used its art to honor its gods and rulers, and record important events.

Fierce serpent heads *framed with feathers are the sign for the god Quetzalcoatl*

Pyramid as *it may have looked when first built*

FEATHERED SERPENT
The stepped pyramid of Quetzalcoatl, the Feathered Serpent, in the ancient Mexican city-state of Teotihuacán, is decorated with sculptures of frightening creatures. The flat background surface of the temple was carved away to make the sculptures stand out from it. This is called a relief sculpture.

Over the years, the paint on the sculptures has worn off

Relief sculpture from the Pyramid of the Feathered Serpent, c. A.D. 200

Carvings of Tlaloc, the goggle-eyed rain god, made up of circles and squares

Amazing Facts

★ **The Olmecs carved huge stone heads weighing up to 20 tonnes. The boulders used to make them were transported about 100 km (60 miles) on rollers and river rafts through jungles.**

Olmec wrestler, 400 B.C.

The Wrestler

The most lively Olmec carved stone sculpture is a small, bearded wrestler. The look of concentration on the figure's face, his firm muscles, and the way he is sitting make it seem as if he has inner energy.

Mayan wall painting showing a religious procession c. A.D. 800

Painted Walls

A picture painted directly onto a wall is called a mural. Murals have been found in the earliest cities of Mexico and northern Central America. They often show grand religious procession.

Eyes made from pearly shell

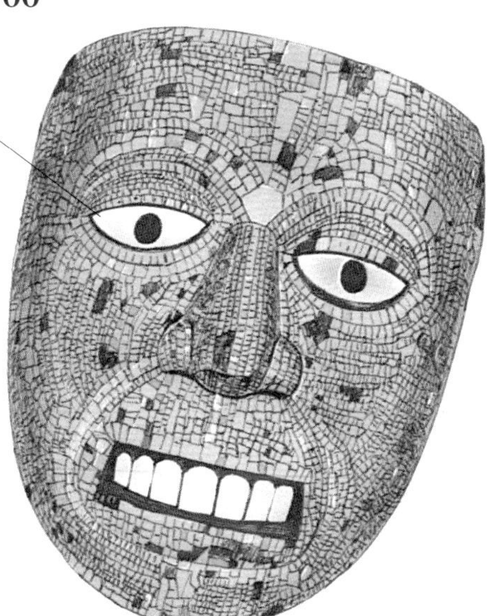

Aztec mask of the god Quetzalcoatl, A.D. 1500

Aztec Mask

The Aztecs ruled most of central Mexico in the mid-1400s A.D.. Turquoise is a blue-green stone that was precious to the Aztecs. They used it to decorate sacred objects, such as masks. The masks were used by priests during religious ceremonies.

FIND OUT MORE
FAMOUS PLACES: Teotihuacán
STORY OF THE PAST: Aztec Empire

Native North American Art

The art of the first North Americans varied according to where and how they lived. The tribes who lived on the prairie grasslands were always traveling to hunt for buffalo, so their art was light and easy to carry. The tribes who lived on the northwest coast were surrounded by trees, so wood carving was their main form of art. They made painted wooden masks and carved huge decorated posts called totem poles.

Carved and painted *figures sit on top of one another as though they have grown out of each other*

Images make *angular patterns*

AMAZING FACTS

★ Each totem pole was carved from a single tree trunk. Some were up to 24 m (80 ft) high – more than 13 times taller than an average man.

TALL STORIES

Native American chiefs from northwest coast tribes put huge poles outdoors to show how important they were. The carved figures on the pole often told how the chief's family began long ago. These totem poles also showed which tribal group the family belonged to.

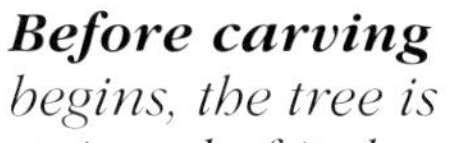

Before carving *begins, the tree is stripped of its bark and branches*

Small model *is copied by the carvers*

Steel tools were *first used by Native American carvers in the A.D. 1800s*

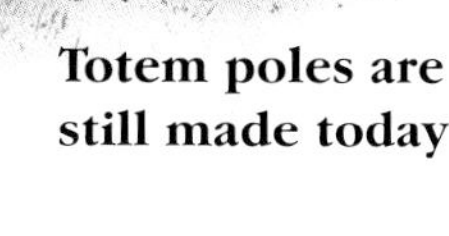

Totem poles are still made today

Totem pole in British Columbia, Canada

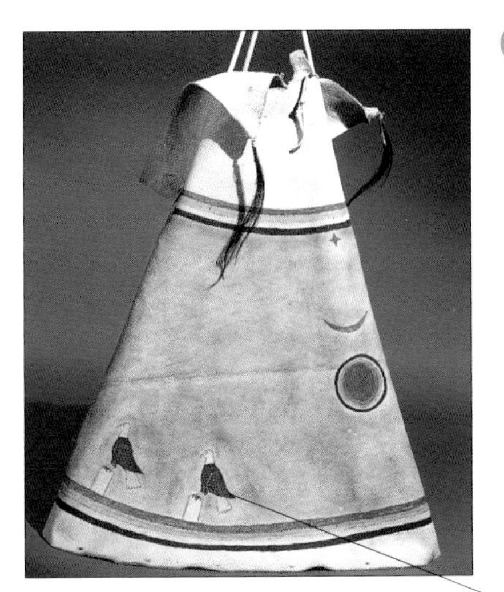

Tepee showing images of Sun, Moon, and Star, and sacred eagles, 1904

Sacred eagle was *believed to carry prayers from Earth to the sky*

PAINTED TEPEES

Many early Native Americans who hunted on the grasslands painted pictures on their war shields, tents called tepees, and clothes. Some of these pictures told stories of tribal events in picture writing. Others were special symbols used by different families. The painters used colored earths for paint. Sticks or animal bones were used as brushes.

Smooth carvings *are small enough to fit in the palm of your hand*

Details such *as the ears are included*

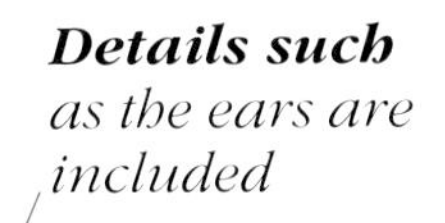

Polar bears made by Inuits from walrus tusks, A.D. 1300s–1400s

INUIT SCULPTURE

The Inuits, from the far north of America, carved bows and arrows with tiny scenes showing animals, hunters, and homes. They also made small ivory sculptures of animals such as seals and polar bears.

Colorful beads can be used to make bold beadwork designs

BEAD EMBROIDERY

Many early Native American tribes decorated their belongings with quill or bead embroidery. At first, porcupines' quills or birds' feathers were dyed and sewn into patterns. Later, colored glass beads from Europe became the main form of decoration.

Beadwork *patterns created using simple shapes*

Beaded pouch in the shape of a turtle

FIND OUT MORE
STORY OF THE PAST: Native Americans
TRAVELERS AND EXPLORERS: America

The Art of Calligraphy

Calligraphy is skillful handwriting that can be admired like a painting. Calligraphers often write with a brush and ink, but sometimes they use a pen or a feather with a flat tip, which is dipped in ink.

Calligraphy is one of the most important kinds of art in China and Japan. It is also highly valued in countries that follow the religion of Islam. The holy book of the Islamic religion, the Qur'an, is written in the Arabic language in a beautiful style of calligraphy.

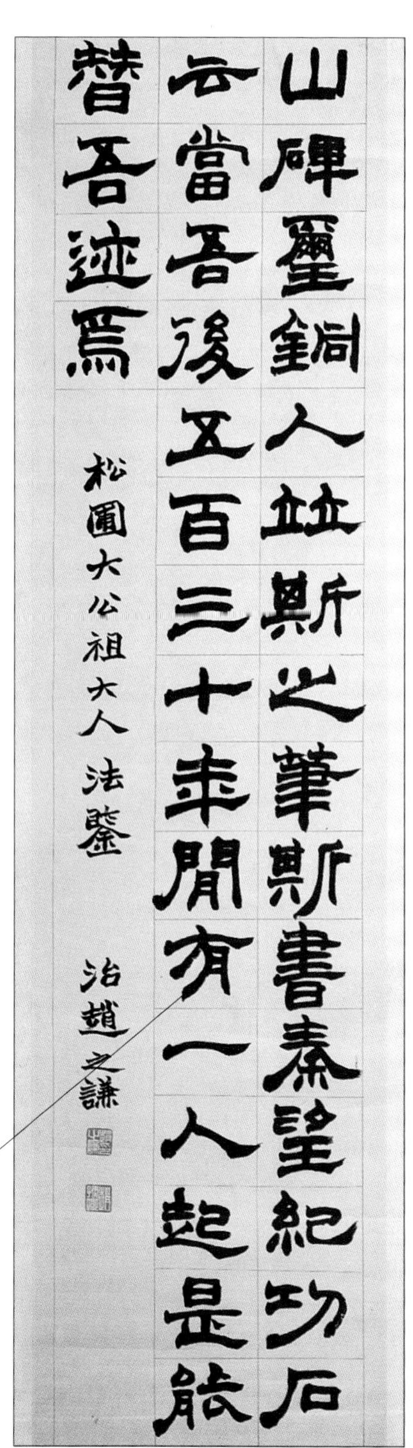

***Characters are** inside an imaginary square that is sometimes sketched in*

Scroll about the art of calligraphy by Zhao Zhiqian, A.D. 1800s

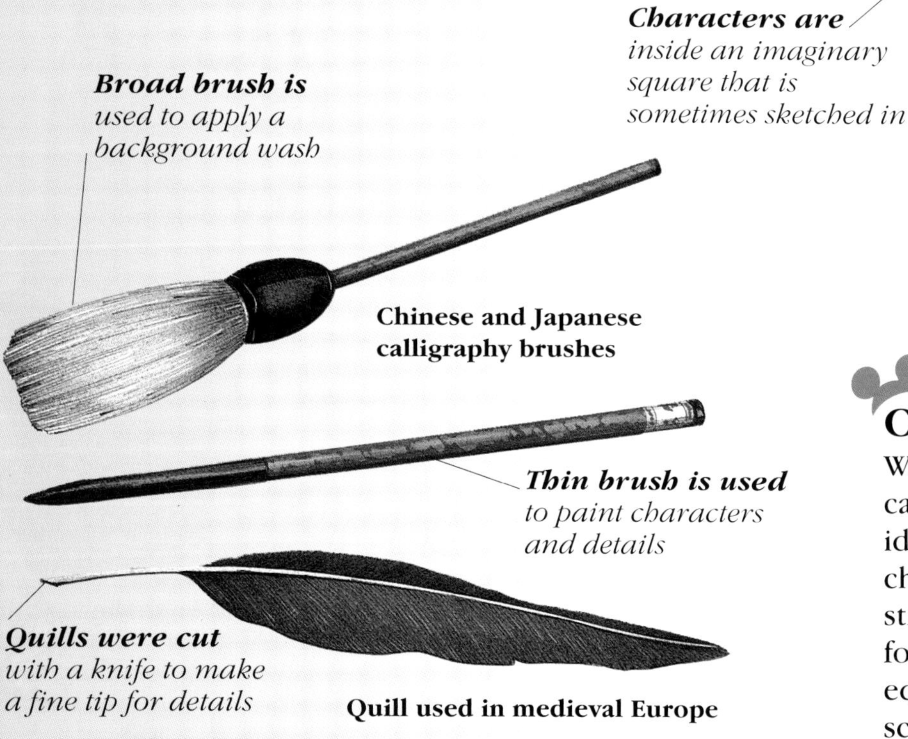

Broad brush is used to apply a background wash
Thin brush is used to paint characters and details
Quills were cut with a knife to make a fine tip for details

Chinese and Japanese calligraphy brushes

Quill used in medieval Europe

CHINESE CALLIGRAPHY

Written Chinese is made up of shapes called characters, which stand for ideas or things. Each line of a character is made with a single brush stroke. A single character can stand for a complicated idea and may be equal to a number of words in the script of other languages.

Sanskrit calligraphy in a horoscope of an Indian prince, c. A.D. 1840

__Letter strokes__
drop downward like curving vines

ISLAMIC CALLIGRAPHY

The Islamic religion does not allow realistic images of living creatures to be shown in religious art. So calligraphy is often used as decoration in mosques, which are the Islamic places of worship.

Mosque lamp decorated with calligraphy from the Qur'an, A.D. 1300s

ELEGANT ALPHABET

The classical Indian language of Sanskrit uses an alphabet called Devanagari. Letters are formed by long, sideways strokes and curving, downward strokes. The gracefulness of the written letters helps to add beauty to the stories they tell.

Illuminated letter by Simone Camaldolese, A.D. 1380–1420

__Curving plant__
and leaf patterns frame the letter M

PICTURE BOOKS

The first books were written out by hand. In Europe, in the A.D. 1500s and 1600s the pages of books were often decorated with capital letters that were illustrated with pictures and patterns. These letters were called illuminated letters. Bits of paper-thin gold were sometimes glued to the pictures to make them look rich and precious.

FIND OUT MORE
COMMUNICATIONS: Calligraphy
GREAT LIVES: Ibn Muqlah

Early Chinese Art

Thousands of years ago, Chinese craftsmen made magnificent bronze containers, with surfaces that were richly decorated with pictures based on animals. The early Chinese also painted graceful pictures on screens and rolls of silk, as well as producing delicate forms of pottery. The many styles of early Chinese art developed under the influence of a series of dynasties, or powerful groups of rulers.

Figure of a deer *at the top of the container*

Figure may be *a magician or a priest, called a shaman*

Container and lid in *the shape of a ferocious tiger that is protecting a human figure*

Squared spirals *make a decorative pattern*

Bronze vessel with a lid, 1100s B.C.

EARLY BRONZES

Bronze vessels, or containers, from Ancient China were used to hold wine and food that was given as an offering to royal ancestors and gods. Some vessels were in the shape of fantastic creatures and decorated with squared spirals called thunder spirals.

According to myth, a crow flies in front of the Sun to end a bad drought

Part of the silk banner showing the heavens painted in bright colors on a dark background, 100s B.C.

SILK PAINTING

Silk and paper are Chinese inventions. Delicate pictures were painted on both using inks and water-based paints. One of the most important early Chinese paintings is a silk banner from a noblewoman's tomb dating from the Qin dynasty. The pictures show the Universe divided into three parts: the heavens, the Earth, and the underworld.

AMAZING FACTS

★ The Chinese have made pottery since prehistoric times. They started to use the potter's wheel before 2000 B.C..

GOLDEN BRONZE

During the Zhou dynasty, c. 1122–256 B.C., elegant bronze containers were decorated with precious metals such as gold and silver. Craftsmen made patterns of shallow hollows in the surface of the bronze to hold the gold or silver. This kind of decoration is called inlay.

***Pattern of** shapes fitted together*

Inlaid container, 400s–200s B.C.

HANDSCROLL PAINTING

Long, narrow handscroll paintings are stored wrapped up in rolls. The roll is opened bit by bit, so that every part of the painting can be studied in turn. One of the oldest handscrolls, by Ku K'ai Chih, is made up of scenes about life in the royal palaces. These include lessons about good palace behavior.

***Figures are** drawn in red and black ink on a plain, flat background*

Handscroll painting called *Admonitions* by Ku K'ai Chih, A.D. 300s

Pottery figure, A.D. 618–907

THREE-COLORED POTTERY

During the Tang dynasty, A.D. 618–907, pottery figures were streaked with three colors of glaze to create bold, splashy patterns. Glaze is a liquid used to decorate pottery. When it hardens, it makes the pottery waterproof.

FIND OUT MORE
GREAT INVENTIONS: Paper
GREAT LIVES: Li Bo

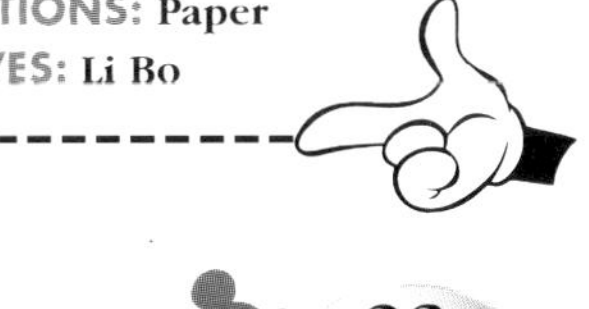

Early Japanese Art

Strangely shaped clay figures called *dogu* are the earliest known Japanese sculptures. These figures are not glazed and show the rough texture or surface of the clay used to make them. The texture of the natural materials used in early Japanese buildings and sculpture was important. Wooden buildings and sculptures were often left partly unpainted to show off the wood. In painting, the different parts of a picture were arranged in an asymmetrical, or uneven, way to attract the eye of the viewer into the picture.

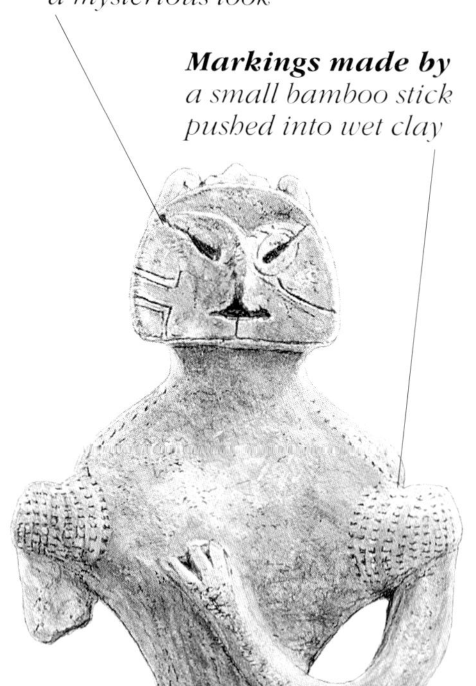
Slit eyes and mouth *give the* dogu *figure a mysterious look*
Markings made by *a small bamboo stick pushed into wet clay*

Dogu **figure, c. 2000 B.C.**

THROW-AWAY CLAY

Dogu figures, made of clay, often have large faces, small hands, and solid bodies. Many were broken on purpose and thrown away. One explanation for this is that the Ancient Japanese may have believed that if a sick person touched a *dogu* and then broke it, the sickness would be cured.

HANIWA SCULPTURES

From A.D. 200 to 500, Japanese sculptors made clay figures, called *haniwa*, of houses, boats, animals, warriors, and servants. These were placed on the mounds that covered the tombs of important people. *Haniwa* have rounded edges but are quite roughly formed.

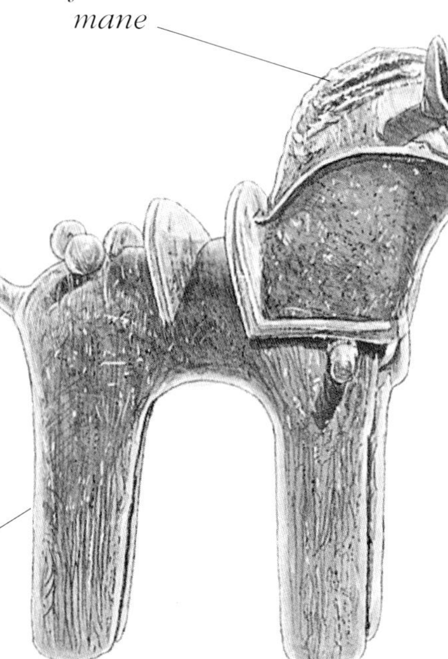
Rough marks *form the horse's mane*
Bold, simple *shapes*

Haniwa **horse, c. A.D. 390**

AMAZING FACTS

★ ***The Tale of Genji*, which was written in the early A.D. 1000s, has been written about in more than 10,000 books in Japan alone.**

Carved wood made to look like rippling muscles
Floating scarf that loops out behind the guardian figure suggests energy and movement

One of the two guardian figures from the Horyu Temple in Nara, southwest Japan, c. A.D. 600s

GIANT GUARDS

Large wooden sculptures were made to decorate Japanese temples. The giant guardian sculptures, called *nio*, stood on either side of a temple gate. The terrifying guardians were often painted red. Their great bulging eyes and fierce expressions were thought to protect the temple and scare away evil spirits.

FAMOUS STORY PAINTINGS

Some of the earliest non-religious paintings from Japan show scenes from a novel about court life called *The Tale of Genji*. The mood of the scenes is shown through colors and lines. Horizontal lines are used to suggest order in calm scenes. Clashing lines and colors are used for scenes in which the characters feel worried or upset.

Detail of a scroll illustrating a scene from *The Tale of Genji*, A.D. 1800s

FIND OUT MORE
GREAT LIVES: Murasaki Shikibu
DANCE, DRAMA, AND MUSIC: Noh

Classical Greek and Roman Art

The Ancient Greeks studied the human body carefully and created wonderfully lifelike statues of people. The bodies they carved show Greek ideas about the beauty and perfection of the human body. The Romans admired and copied Greek art, but they also created works of their own including colorful frescoes, or wall paintings, and mosaics.

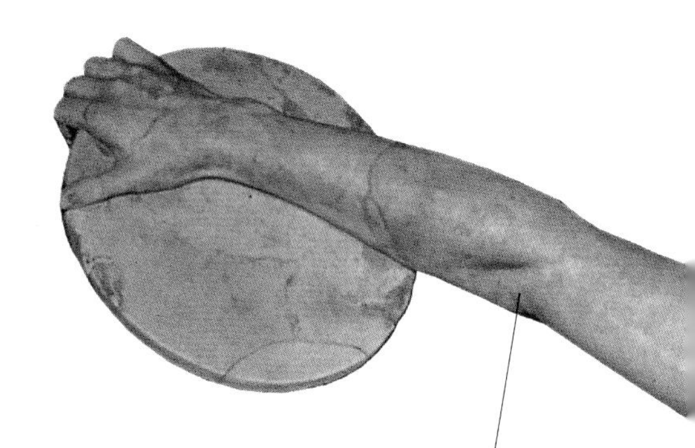

Throwing arm *looks strong and powerful*

Muscular body *is coiled tightly, ready to unwind and hurl the discus through the air*

Shape of the *calf muscle is accurately carved*

Greek hero *Achilles plunging his spear into an Amazon queen*

Wine jar by Exekias, c. 540 B.C.

GREEK STATUES

Like many Greek statues, *The Discus Thrower* is free-standing and carved on all sides. It was made in bronze, then later copied by the Romans in marble. Greek sculptors also created statues of their gods and goddesses, which showed realistic detail as well as movement and feeling.

POTTERY PAINTING

Very few early Greek paintings have survived. But many paintings can be seen on vases and jars, called amphorae, used for storing oil and wine. The pictures show scenes from Greek myths or everyday life.

AMAZING FACTS

★ **The Greeks made a statue of the goddess Athena that was so tall it could be seen from 16 km (10 miles) away.**

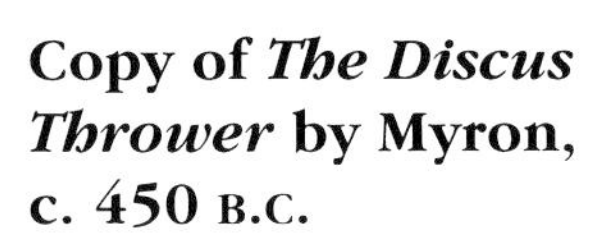

Copy of *The Discus Thrower* by Myron, c. 450 B.C.

Head forms the *end part of the twisted, S-shaped curve of the body*

CARVED FRIEZE

The Parthenon is a famous Greek temple built in Athens about 7,000 years ago. A frieze, or band of relief sculpture, was carved around the top. The top part of the frieze sticks out more than the lower part so that it can be seen from the ground below.

Part of the Parthenon frieze, showing the procession honoring the goddess Athena's birthday, 447–432 B.C.

Roman wall painting of a coastal scene, near Pompeii, first century A.D.

ROMAN WALL PAINTING

The inside walls of grand Roman houses were often painted to show scenes from myths and history, as well as landscapes and portraits. Borders were added around some wall paintings to look like frames.

ROMAN MOSAICS

Rich Romans had the floors of their homes decorated with mosaics. These pictures were made up of tiny cubes of colored stone or glass laid in wet plaster. Sometimes they looked like paintings.

Trays were *used to hold the tiny pieces of stone or glass*

Making a Roman-style mosaic

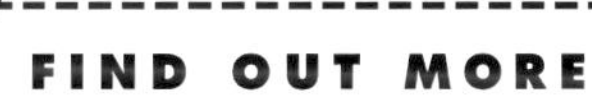

FIND OUT MORE
SPORT: Olympic Games
STORY OF THE PAST: Ancient Greece

Making Sculpture

A sculpture can be made in many ways. It can be cast, using a mold, or shaped from something soft, such as clay. It can be made by cutting or chipping away at something hard like stone, or it can be built up by fixing together different materials such as plastic, glass, and wire.

Bronze is often used for casting because it melts when it is heated and hardens when it cools. Wet clay hardens when it is baked, or fired, in an oven called a kiln. After firing, clay can be painted with a decorative colored glaze, and then fired again.

Clay is a sticky earth that can be shaped

CASTING A BRONZE STATUE

1 A plaster statue, or core, is carefully sculpted. Next a wet plaster mold is added around the core.

When wet *plaster dries, it becomes hard*

Bronze will *be the same thickness as the layer of wax*

2 The hard mold is cut in half and removed from the core. The inside is coated with wax. The two halves are then put back together with the core inside.

Pouring pot *is used to pour the liquid bronze metal into the mold*

3 The mold is heated so the wax inside melts. Hot, liquid bronze is poured into the space between the core and the mold.

Mold is held *together with clay and metal bands*

PAPER SCULPTURES

Papier mâché is made from paper mashed in glue or from sheets of paper pasted together. As the glue dries, the paper hardens. Papier mâché sculptures are often built around a wire skeleton that is left inside the sculpture. Once the papier mâché art is dry, it can be painted. Papier mâché art is popular in Mexico, China, India, and Japan.

Mexican papier mâché skull

CARVING MARBLE

Marble is a popular, hard stone used in buildings, monuments, and sculptures. To make a marble statue, a sculptor roughs out the shape with a hammer and chisel. Then chisels and drills are used to make the shape clearer and smoother. Finally, the surface is polished with a pumice stone.

Small plaster *model, or maquette, of the statue helps the sculptor*

Marble busts are often *made as head-and-shoulder portraits of wealthy or famous people*

Marble occurs in *different colors and patterns. Statues are usually made from white marble*

Sculptor working with a hammer and chisel

After the plaster *has been removed, extra details are added with a chisel*

4 The bronze cools and the plaster is broken away to reveal the statue. The statue takes on exactly the same shape as the wax.

FIND OUT MORE
GREAT INVENTIONS: Bronze
SCIENCE ALL AROUND US: Materials

Traditional African Art

An amazing range of bold sculptures was made in Ancient Africa. Wood, stone, metal, and clay sculptures were the main form of art. These sculptures were of figures, masks, decorated boxes, and objects for religious use. Some sculptures have features, such as the eyes, that are bigger and simpler than they are in life. Others are more lifelike and may have been portraits of important people. Sculptures were used in religious and magic ceremonies.

Nok head in terra cotta, c. 500 B.C.

TERRA COTTA SCULPTURE

Some of the oldest African sculptures were made in a type of clay called terra cotta, by the Nok people of southern Nigeria. Many Nok sculptures are of human figures, with holes made in the wet clay for the nostrils, pupils, and mouths. These holes made the head look real and stopped it cracking when it was fired in a kiln or oven to become hard.

Wooden masks with *heart-shaped faces are found in central and western Africa*

Shapes and lines *of the mask are bold and carefully balanced*

African masks, A.D. 1800s

MAKING FACES

Masks were made to be worn during dances and ceremonies. The ceremonies celebrated important events, such as initiation, when a young person was old enough to become part of the adult world.

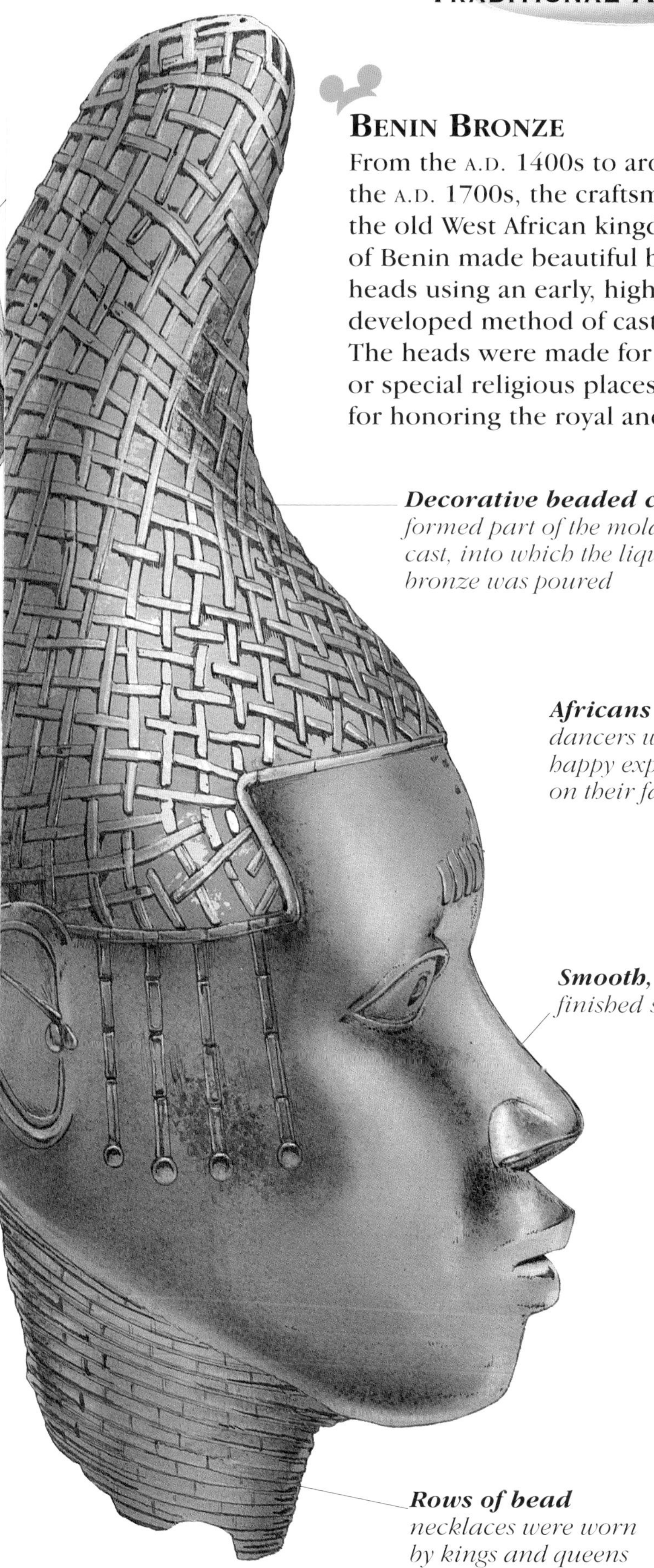

BENIN BRONZE

From the A.D. 1400s to around the A.D. 1700s, the craftsmen of the old West African kingdom of Benin made beautiful bronze heads using an early, highly developed method of casting. The heads were made for shrines or special religious places used for honoring the royal ancestors.

Decorative beaded cap *formed part of the mold, or cast, into which the liquid bronze was poured*

Smooth, even *finished surface*

Rows of bead *necklaces were worn by kings and queens*

Benin head of Queen Mother 50 cm (20 in) high, c. A.D 1500–50

AMAZING FACTS

★ **In Benin, only the king could order bronze sculptures to be made.**

★ **In some dances, African masks are worn on the top of the head facing toward the sky.**

Africans carved *dancers with calm, happy expressions on their faces*

Cameroon dancing couple, A.D. 1800s

WOODEN DANCERS

Wooden sculptures from Cameroon have a real sense of movement. They are carved as if frozen in the middle of their dance, with knees bent and arms mid-swing.

FIND OUT MORE
DANCE, DRAMA, AND MUSIC: Cameroon
STORY OF THE PAST: Benin Bronzes

Hindu Art

Hinduism began over 5,000 years ago in India. Stories about the exciting lives of powerful gods and goddesses are the main subject of Hindu religious art. Sculptures and paintings are made mostly for temples and shrines. The poses of the gods, animals, and objects in Hindu art all have special religious meanings, which teach about living a good life. The figures are lively, and scenes are crowded with people and animals.

Shiva has a *calm expression that contrasts with his moving body*

One hand holds *a drum for beating out the rhythm of his creative dance*

Shiva's four arms *are used to show his different powers*

Shiva's right *foot stamps on the demon of ignorance*

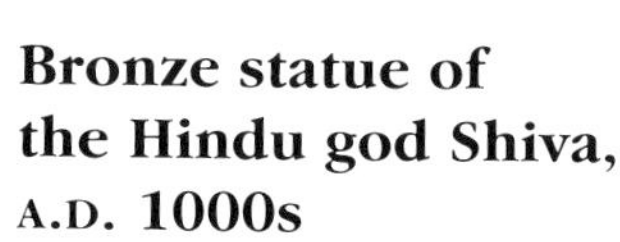

Bronze statue of the Hindu god Shiva, A.D. 1000s

DANCING SHIVA

The god Shiva rules over creation and destruction and symbolizes fertility. He is also called the Lord of the Dance and is often shown in bronze sculptures as a dancing figure. His dance represents the energy that flows through the Universe, causing birth and death and controlling the seasons.

AMAZING FACTS

★ **Before paper was introduced into India, artists often painted on palm leaves that were later bound into books.**

Arjuna's Penance, or *The Descent of the Ganges*, rock carving, Mahabalipuram, India, A.D. 600s

All creatures *face toward the split in the rock*

ROCK STORY

In southern India, there is a huge rock covered with ancient carvings that tells the story of how India's holy River Ganges fell to Earth from heaven. In the carvings, gods and creatures have gathered from everywhere to see the miracle. Water from a tank above flows down a split in the rock on special occasions to re-create the flowing river.

COLORFUL TEMPLES

Many Hindu temples in southern India are guarded by towers called gopura. They are covered with hundreds of images of gods and goddesses to protect the temple from evil. The broad strips of relief are often brightly painted.

Detail of a gopura, Sri Meenakshi Temple, Madurai, India, c. A.D. 1200s

Circle represents the *Universe Shiva creates*

Detail of a painting featuring the Hindu god Vishnu, A.D. 1700s

Flames show *Shiva's destruction of the world and the Universe*

TINY PAINTINGS

The Rajputs were important Hindu nobles, who ruled parts of northern India from about A.D. 600 to 1500. The artists who worked at their courts created tiny colorful paintings called miniatures. The paintings could measure as little as 8 cm (3 in) across.

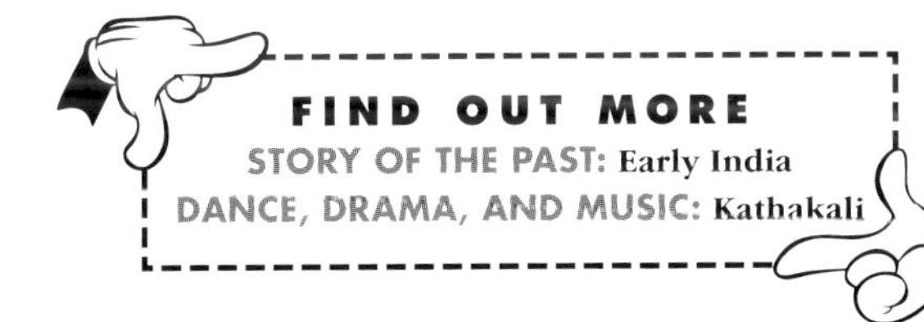

FIND OUT MORE
STORY OF THE PAST: Early India
DANCE, DRAMA, AND MUSIC: Kathakali

The Renaissance

The Renaissance, or "rebirth," was an exciting time for new ideas and art in Europe. It was based on the rediscovery of classical Greek and Roman art, literature, and architecture. From the A.D. 1400s to the end of the A.D. 1600s, artists started to paint realistic landscapes, portraits of real people, and scenes from daily life. Sculptors also tried to copy classical skill and style in their work by careful study of the human body.

School of Athens **by Raphael (real name Raffaello Sanzio), 1510–11**

AMAZING FACTS

★ **Michelangelo's *David* is carved from a block of marble that had been rejected by another sculptor because he thought it was no good.**

USING PERSPECTIVE

Looking at the painting *School of Athens* by the Italian artist Raphael is like looking inside a real building that stretches back into real space, behind the picture's frame. Many other Renaissance artists used perspective, a way of representing objects in relation to one another, to make their paintings seem three dimensional.

MICHELANGELO'S *DAVID*

David was a young hero who, according to the Bible, killed a giant named Goliath. Italian artist Michelangelo's statue of *David* shows the influence of classical Greek and Roman sculpture. But the Renaissance approach can also be seen in the powerful feelings shown on *David*'s face and his accurately modeled muscles.

Face shows realistic *features and emotion*

Even small details, *such as the tendons on* David's *hand, have been carved*

Skillfully carved *stomach muscles show that Michelangelo studied human anatomy*

David **by Michelangelo Buonarroti, 1501–1504**

Figures appear *smaller as they get farther away, to show depth*

Raphael painted himself *in his picture of an imaginary gathering of Ancient Greek scientists and thinkers*

Eyes seem *to follow you around*

Pattern on *Mona Lisa's dress is delicately painted*

Mona Lisa **by Leonardo da Vinci, 1503–1506**

MONA LISA

Italian artist Leonardo da Vinci created *Mona Lisa*'s mysterious smile by softening the corners of her eyes and mouth with shadows. The misty landscape behind also adds to the famous painting's sense of mystery.

FIND OUT MORE
GREAT LIVES: Michelangelo
STORY OF THE PAST: The Renaissance

BAROQUE SCULPTURE

Baroque is a dramatic and decorative style of art and architecture that began in Italy in the 1600s. Many Baroque sculptures decorate churches. Bernini's sculpture shows St. Teresa having a religious vision. The deep folds in Teresa's clothes give the sculpture movement and depth. Both Teresa and the angel look like actors under a spotlight.

Golden rays lit from a window above draw attention to the sculpture

Ecstasy of St. Teresa by Giovanni Lorenzo Bernini, 1645–52

All Sorts of Paints

There are many different kinds of paints that can be painted onto many different kinds of surfaces. Each kind of paint creates different effects, so the artist has to choose which one will work best for each new painting.

The basic ingredients in paint are pigments, which give the paint its color. The kind of paint depends on what the pigments are mixed with. Slow-drying oil paints are made of pigments mixed with vegetable oil. Watercolor paints are made of pigments, water, and gum arabic, which helps the paint stick to paper.

Canvas was painted *with a "ground," a base coat of glue and colored pigment, before painting started*
Flexibility and *texture of canvas make it a good surface on which to use oil paints*
Artist's *assistant*
Easel supports *canvas*
Mortar and pestle *for grinding the pigments used to make paint*

Painting with oil paints in a Renaissance studio

Watercolors allow white paper to show through the transparent paint

PAINTING IN OILS

Oil paints became popular in the West during the Renaissance. Artists liked them because they could be put on in layers, to build up deep colors. They also gave a smooth, shiny appearance with no brush strokes showing. This made it easier to paint lifelike people and places.

Model sits still while her portrait is painted

Both the picture and the way of painting are called fresco

Dolphin fresco in Knossos, Crete, 1450 –1400 B.C.

FRESCO PAINTING

A fresco is a painting made on wet plaster. Plaster is often used to cover ceilings or walls. The paint mixes with the wet plaster and when it dries, it becomes part of the ceiling or wall.

GORGEOUS GOUACHE

Gouache is a watercolor paint with white pigment added to make the color brighter and less see-through. During the rule of the Mughals in India, gouache was used to make book paintings. Once dry, the paintings were put face down on marble and rubbed with a stone to make them shine.

Mughal painting, A.D. 1700s

NATURAL PIGMENTS

For thousands of years all pigments used to color paint came from plants, animals, or colored rocks. Today most pigments are made with chemicals.

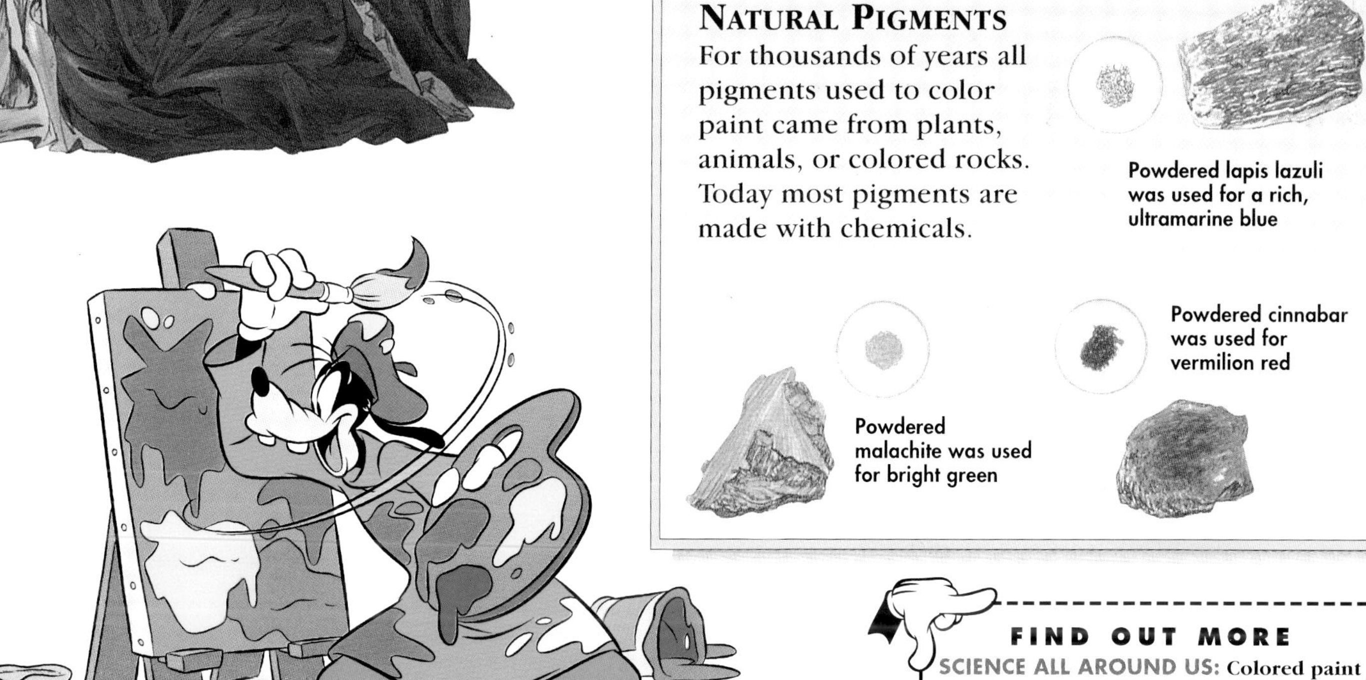

Powdered lapis lazuli was used for a rich, ultramarine blue

Powdered cinnabar was used for vermilion red

Powdered malachite was used for bright green

FIND OUT MORE

SCIENCE ALL AROUND US: Colored paint
PLANT LIFE: Plant products

Japanese Prints

The most famous Japanese woodblock prints were made from the A.D. 1600s to the late A.D. 1800s. This was a period of change in Japan, when art became less formal and more lifelike. These prints show scenes from daily life or from entertainments, such as the theater. The prints were called *ukiyo-e*, which means "pictures of a floating world." These prints were first used to illustrate books. But when people liked the pictures, publishers produced the prints separately.

Foam of wave looks like *claws ready to pounce on the men in the boat below*

Shape of wave matches *the snow-capped Mount Fuji in the distance*

Woodblock print *In the Well of the Great Wave of Kanagawa* by Katsushika Hokusai, c. 1831

PICTURE TO PRINT

For each woodblock print, the artist first drew an original picture in color on paper. Then a copy of the picture was stuck onto a block of wood and carved along the lines of one color so that they stood out. A separate block was carved for each color in the picture. Finally, the blocks were brushed with different colored inks and printed one at a time to make the whole color picture.

Mount Fuji is *Japan's most important mountain*

Heads of the men *in the boat look tiny compared to the giant waves*

STAGE STAR PRINTS

Most Japanese prints show pictures of elegant women, famous actors, birds, flowers, or outdoor scenes of Japan. The actor prints were bought by theatergoers just as people today buy posters of their favorite pop or movie stars.

Watanabe Discovers the Beautiful No Tsuna **by Ando Hiroshige, 1845–48**

PRINTS TO DECORATE

Some prints were designed to be printed on fans. Others were made to be cut out and pasted onto screens as decoration or onto the sides of paper lanterns, so that they stood out when the lanterns were lit.

Backgrounds *were plain and uncluttered*

The actor Fujikawa Tomokichi II **by Toyokuni Utagawa, c. 1811**

BOLD SHAPES AND COLORS

Japanese woodblock prints have a flat arrangement of strong shapes and bold, solid colors. When Western artists saw these prints for the first time in the 1850s, they greatly admired them and began using bold designs and colors in their own work.

Print is specially *designed to fit the curved shape of the fan*

Fan with woodblock print, 1600s

AMAZING FACTS

★ So many prints were made in the 1800s that Japanese traders even used them to wrap up goods such as tea cups.

FIND OUT MORE
GREAT INVENTIONS: Woodblock printing
DANCE, DRAMA, AND MUSIC: Fans

Abstract Art

An abstract painting or sculpture is one that does not try to represent people, animals, or anything else you might recognize from the real world. Instead, it tries to suggest meaning through shapcs, lines, and colors. The first abstract paintings were made in about 1910. Before that, artists had only used abstract shapes to decorate things such as buildings and books.

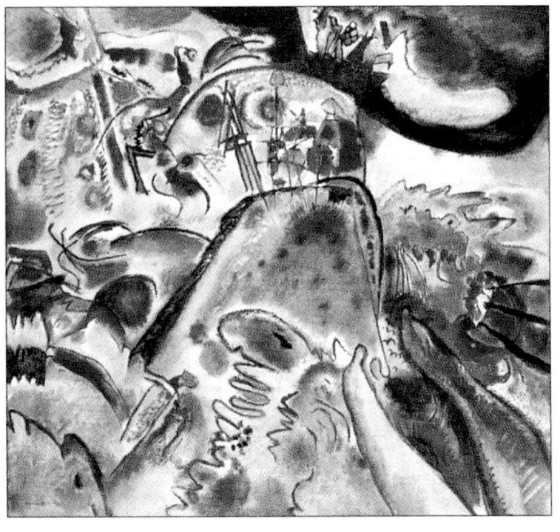

Small Pleasures by Wassily Kandinsky, 1913

ABSTRACT PAINTING

One of the first abstract paintings was made by the Russian artist Wassily Kandinsky. He believed that the colors and shapes he put in his paintings could affect people's feelings.

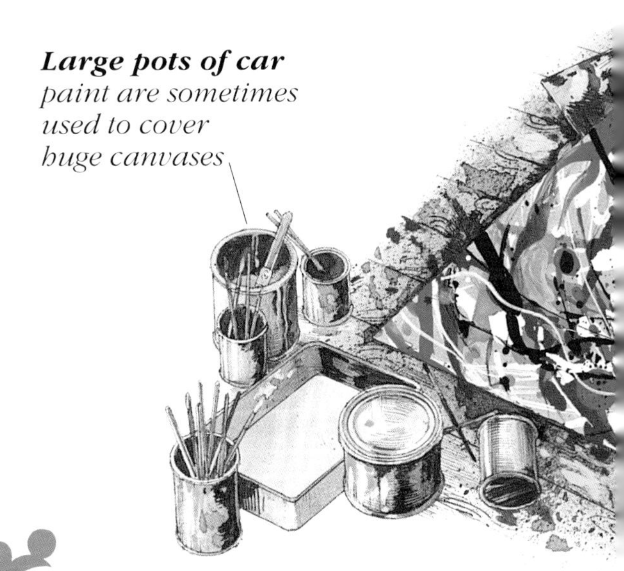

Large pots of car *paint are sometimes used to cover huge canvases*

DRIPS AND SPLASHES

In a drip painting, the paint is dripped, splashed, or poured onto a large canvas, which is often stretched out on the floor. American Jackson Pollock was one of the first drip painters. He is also called an "action painter" because when he painted, he moved over and around the canvas, spilling paint and whirling his arms as though he were dancing.

BLOWING IN THE WIND

A mobile is a sculpture that is made up of parts that move in the breeze. In the 1930s, the American sculptor Alexander Calder became famous for his mobiles made out of carefully balanced wire rods and flat metal shapes.

Alexander Calder with models of his mobiles, 1967

ABSTRACT SCULPTURE

British sculptor Barbara Hepworth got ideas for her abstract sculptures from the shells, rocks, and leaves near her seaside home in England. Many of her smooth, curving sculptures were made to be seen outdoors.

Holes allow the viewer to see through the sculpture

Oval Sculpture by Barbara Hepworth, 1943

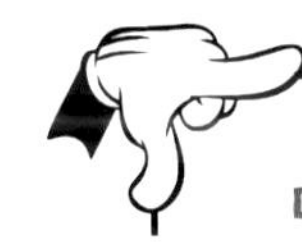

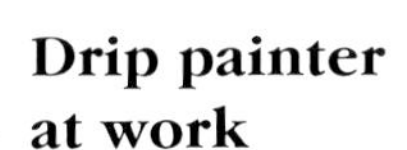

Drip painter at work

Stick brush does not touch *the canvas. Instead paint falls from the stick onto the painting*

AMAZING FACTS

★ Jackson Pollock sometimes made interesting looping patterns in his drip paintings by riding a bicycle over them while they were still wet.

FIND OUT MORE
DANCE, DRAMA, AND MUSIC:
Theatre of the Absurd

Glossary of Key Words

Abstract: An artwork that does not show recognizable things from the real world, but instead consists of patterns of shapes, lines, and colors.

Ancestor: A member of a person's family or race who lived many generations before.

Archeologist: A person who finds out how people lived by examining the objects they left behind.

Art: The creation of things such as paintings, drawings, and sculptures.

Bronze: A metal made by mixing copper and tin, often used in sculptures.

Bust: A model or sculpture of a person's head, shoulders, and chest.

Canvas: A tightly woven cloth, usually made of cotton, linen, or hemp, upon which a painting may be created.

Casting: A way of making a sculpture by pouring hot metal into a mold and leaving it to cool and harden.

c. or circa: An approximate date. For example c. A.D. 1000 means about A.D. 1000.

Classical: From or relating to Ancient Greek or Roman times. Classical also refers to art that is well balanced.

Clay: Heavy earth that becomes soft when wet and hardens when it is baked or dried. Clay is used to make pottery and sculptures.

Cubism: A style of art in which figures and objects are broken up into simple shapes, and arranged in a pattern so that the original objects are often still recognizable.

Decorate: To make something look attractive by adding colors, shapes, or patterns.

Design: A decorative pattern of lines and shapes.

Dreamtime: An ancient time in Australian Aboriginal beliefs, when the world was created by spirit beings.

Dye: A substance that can change the color of things such as paper, cloth, skin, and hair.

Embroidery: Ornate sewing that decorates a piece of cloth.

Figure: Word for a person or an animal in a work of art.

Frieze: A band of sculpture or decoration at the top of a wall, building, or piece of furniture.

Graffiti: Scribbled writing or drawings on walls or sidewalks.

Image: The picture of a person, animal, or object made in a painting, photograph, or sculpture.

Impressionism: A style of painting that gives the impression, or idea, of a subject, especially by using the changing effects of light.

Landscape: A painting of the natural scenery of a place.

Material: The substance from which objects of art are made, such as clay or paint.

Medieval: Belonging to the historical period c. A.D. 500–1500. Also known as the Middle Ages.

Mold: A container used to give shape to a material such as melted bronze or clay.

Object: Anything that you can see or touch.

Offering: A gift given to a god, often during a religious ceremony.

Perspective: The art of drawing so that some objects appear to be farther away than others.

Portrait: A picture of a person.

Prehistoric: The time before history was written down.

Realistic: Seeming like real life. A realistic painting shows objects as they really appear.

Renaissance: A period in Western history, c. 1300s–1600s, when artists celebrated the human body in lifelike paintings and sculptures.

Represent: To show or stand for something.

Sacred: Honored because the object or idea is thought to be holy, or religious.

Script: A system of writing, for example Chinese or Roman.

Sculpture: A figure or object carved or shaped from a material such as stone, wood, or clay.

Self-portrait: A picture by an artist of him or herself.

Shrine: A place or structure dedicated to a holy person, saint, or god.

Statue: A sculpture of a person, animal, or object.

Subject: Something shown or represented in a painting, photograph, or sculpture.

Symbol: An image in which something, usually from real life, refers to something else. For example, an empty throne is one of the symbols of Buddha.

Three-dimensional (3D): Having width, height, and depth.

Traditional: Handed down from generation to generation.

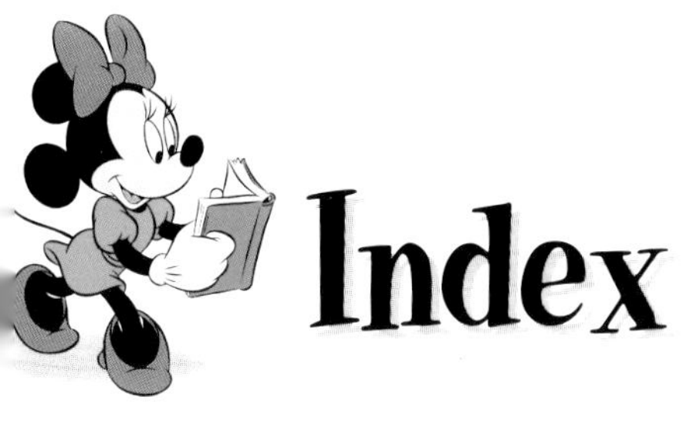

Index

(*see* **Famous Places** for a full index to your complete set of books)